Where Is the Taj Mahal?

by Dorothy and Thomas Hoobler

illustrated by John Hinderliter

Grosset & Dunlap
An Imprint of Penguin Random House

For Sharad and Bharati Banavadikar, who showed us the wonders of the Taj Mahal—DH and TH

For Ruby, you keep reading them and I'll keep making them—JH

GROSSET & DUNLAP
Penguin Young Readers Group
An Imprint of Penguin Random House LLC

Library of Congress Cataloging-in-Publication Data is available.

ISBN 9780399542145 (paperback) 10 9 8 7 6 5 4 3 2 1
ISBN 9780399542152 (library binding) 10 9 8 7 6 5 4 3 2 1

Contents

Where Is the Taj Mahal?

Each year more than two million visitors arrive in the city of Agra, India. Some have traveled from the other side of the world. They have come to see one of the world's most famous buildings.

The Taj Mahal.

Its white marble dome shimmers in sunlight and sparkles when the moon shines. Many believe it is the most beautiful building in the world.

The Taj does not stand alone. It is part of a group of buildings and gardens that occupies forty-two acres. It stands on the banks of the Yamuna River, a major river of northern India.

People who don't know anything about the

Taj Mahal may think it is a palace. But it was not built for people to live in. The Taj is a tomb. It contains the bodies of a ruler named Shah Jahan and his wife Mumtaz Mahal. The name Taj Mahal is a shortened form of her name.

Shah Jahan adored his wife. When she died giving birth to their fourteenth child, Shah Jahan vowed to build a magnificent tomb that would show his undying love for her . . . and he did.

Modern India

Even though it was built nearly four hundred years ago, the Taj Mahal has become a symbol of modern India, the world's largest democracy. India has 1.2 billion people, the second-largest population in the world. Only China's is larger. Agra, where the Taj Mahal is located, is about 130 miles south of New Delhi, the nation's capital.

India is the birthplace of several different religions. Many languages are spoken within its borders. In the past, these differences prevented India from becoming united. Today, most of its people take great pride in their country's different traditions and cultures.

CHAPTER 1
A Joyous Childhood

The ruler later known as Shah Jahan was the fifth emperor of the Mogul dynasty, which ruled much of what is present-day India from 1526 to 1858. At its height of power, the Mogul Empire included parts of Pakistan and Afghanistan.

The first six rulers of the Mogul Empire were probably the richest in the world at that time. European travelers spread the stories of the Moguls' fabulous wealth and power. The rulers of Europe admired the splendor and luxury of the Moguls. In the 1600s and 1700s the term "Great Mogul" meant the kind of powerful ruler that European monarchs wanted to be as well.

The Moguls' reputation for wealth made the name *mogul* a synonym for a wealthy person—as

it still is today. Those who reach great success in business, and particularly the movie industry, are called moguls.

As for Shah Jahan, everything about his birth in 1592 seemed lucky. The year was 1000 in the Islamic calendar, and the month was the same month as Muhammad's birthday. (Muhammad was the prophet who began the religion of Islam.)

Islam

The religion of Islam was started by a man named Muhammad in the seventh century AD. He lived in Arabia. The holy book of Islam is called the Koran. Like Judaism and Christianity, Islam teaches that there is only one God. Muslims (those who believe in Islam) believe that Jesus and Moses were prophets, like Muhammad.

Muslims regard Mecca, a city in Saudi Arabia, as holy. Five times a day, Muslims turn in the direction of Mecca and pray. Muslims try to make a *pilgrimage*, or trip, to Mecca at least once in their lifetimes.

In ancient times, Muslims spread their religion over a large area, from North Africa to central Asia. The Mogul rulers were Muslims. However, they allowed their subjects to follow other religions.

At his birth, the future emperor was given the name Khurram. It meant "joyous." Just before he was born, a fortune-teller made a prediction to his grandfather's first wife, Ruqaiya. He said that this child would have a great future and be "more resplendent than the sun."

Ruqaiya had no children of her own. She wanted to raise a future emperor. So when Khurram was six days old, he was taken from his mother and given to Ruqaiya. The mother was paid with rubies and pearls for her loss. From then on Ruqaiya was in charge of the child's upbringing.

Like all the children and grandchildren of the Mogul ruler, Khurram grew up in the palace harem. (The word *harem* comes from an Arabic word meaning "sacred" or "forbidden.") This was where the women and children of the household stayed, apart from men. The emperor's wives lived there, along with his mother, aunts, nieces, and young children. Female servants lived there, too. Even the harem guards were women who were trained to use a bow and arrow. The only grown man to enter was the emperor himself. He slept there. It was also where he kept his most important papers.

The Harem

The harem was a huge place, offering all the comfort and luxury of a royal village. Besides schools and nurseries, there were markets, laundries, kitchens, playgrounds, and baths. Entertainment included fireworks, snake charmers, dancing bears, and gazelle fights. A favorite pastime was making perfumes. The women of the harem even invested in businesses in the outside world. It was a Muslim custom for a woman to cover her face with a veil when she appeared in public. Inside the harem, however, women could take off their veils.

Khurram's education began when he was four years, four months, and four days old. (Four was considered a lucky number.) He went to school in a mosque (an Islamic house of worship). He studied religion, arts, literature, and history. He learned all about his family and Mogul ancestors.

From a young age, Khurram loved beautiful things. He liked to drench himself and his clothes with perfume and play with precious gems. But he also learned how to be a warrior. Hunting and fighting were part of his life as well.

Khurram was always close to his grandfather Akbar, the emperor. Akbar took him to battles to improve his skills with a bow and to learn to ride a horse. At the age of nine, the boy was allowed to join the war council.

When Akbar lay dying, Khurram refused to leave his bedside. Nine days after Akbar's death, Khurram's father was proclaimed emperor in the Red Fort at Agra. He took the name Jahangir, which means "Seizer of the World."

The Red Fort

Akbar was a great builder. In Agra he built the enormous Red Fort. It served as a palace, a government building, and living quarters for the ruler's family and courtiers. It was one and a half miles around its double walls. Akbar showed off his strength by running around it holding a man under each arm. Here he held court and took petitions from

his subjects. One of his ministers wrote, "A castle of red sandstone, the like of which no traveler has ever seen, has been created by the emperor. The fort alone contains five hundred wonderful stone buildings."

Thousands of people lived here, as well as animals such as elephants, lions, and camels. The fort would also play an important role in the lives of both Shah Jahan and Mumtaz Mahal.

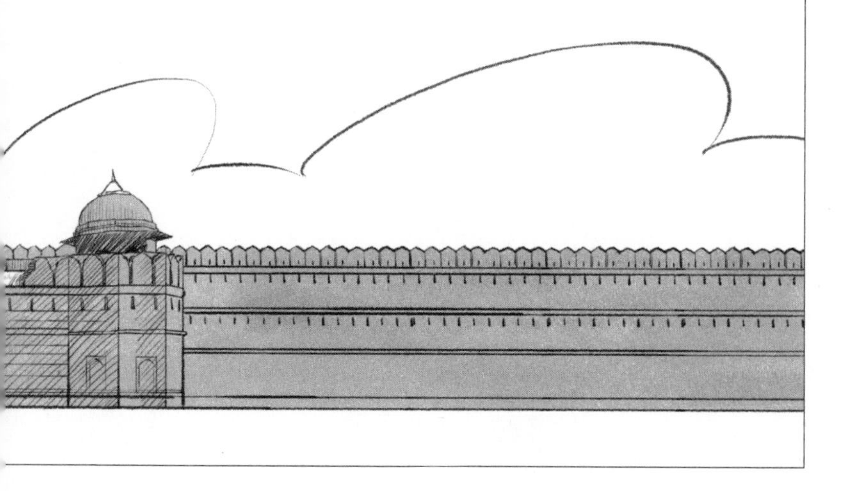

Khurram continued with his education and training. He showed great talent in the skills of war, the arts, and architecture. But when he was fifteen, his life changed.

What happened?

He met a girl and fell in love.

CHAPTER 2
Young Lovers

During the New Year holiday season, the women of the palace always held a fair in the Red Fort. They sold things for charity. It was one of the few times when Muslim women could be seen in public without their veils.

Helping at one of the booths was a fourteen-year-old girl. She came from an important family, but she was not a princess. Khurram stopped at her booth and bought a large piece of glass shaped like a diamond. He is said to have paid ten thousand rupees, an incredibly high price.

But he would have paid almost anything just to please the beautiful young girl. The very next day, he asked his father for permission to marry her. His father agreed on one condition: Khurram had to wait five years and during that time, he could not see the girl. Not even once.

Many things happened during those years. Khurram's father arranged for him to marry a Persian princess. (He was allowed to have four wives.) And even though he had two older brothers, Khurram had been named heir to the throne. That meant he would be emperor after Jahangir died. Becoming the heir entitled Khurram to use a red tent. This honor usually went to the oldest son of the ruler. Khurram was also made a commander in the army.

During these years, the girl from the fair always remained his true love. When the five years were up, Khurram reminded his father of his promise. And his father remained true

to his word. On March 27, 1612, a day chosen as important for a happy marriage, the young couple were wed.

Most people in India were Hindus. So even though the ruling family members were Muslims, much of the ceremony followed Hindu customs. The groom went to the bride's house on the back of an elephant. (Ganesh is a Hindu god with the head of an elephant. He blesses the beginnings of important projects.)

Hinduism

Hinduism is an ancient religion of India, though many followers think of it not as a religion but as a way of life (*dharma*). Even so, Hindus believe in numerous gods and goddesses. There are many stories about the adventures of the gods and goddesses. Countless temples are decorated with statues of them. Today, most Indians still follow some form of Hinduism.

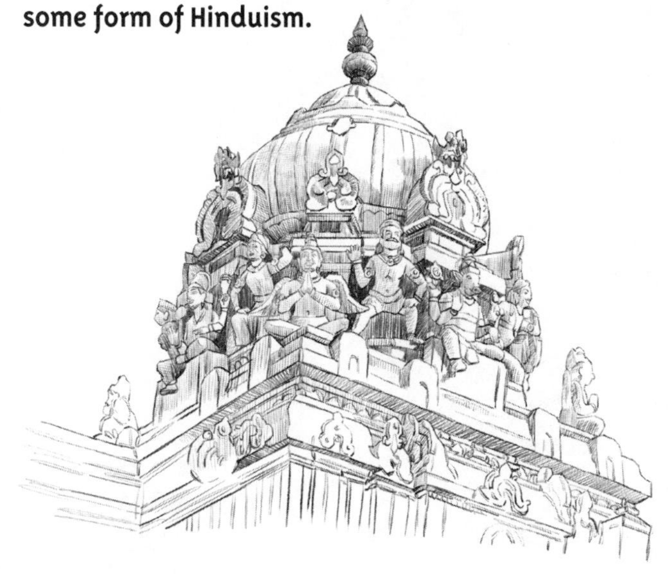

Once the groom arrived, women who hid their faces behind a curtain painted designs on his hands. These were supposed to bring good luck. Khurram's father tied a wedding tiara made of pearls on his son's head.

The bride was asked if she agreed to the marriage. She gave her consent, and the families exchanged gifts. Khurram rinsed his hands in rosewater and drank water to show that he, too, agreed to the marriage. Khurram gave his bride the title Mumtaz Mahal, which means "Chosen One of the Palace." The feasting, with gala parades and fireworks, went on for a month.

It was just the beginning of a wonderful life together.

CHAPTER 3
Always Together

Khurram's father, Jahangir, had little interest in waging war and conquering new lands. He was more interested in painting and natural history. He also drank heavily and took drugs. He let one of his wives run the government.

It was up to Khurram to keep the empire from falling apart. He commanded the armies and often led troops to put down rebellions.

Women hardly ever went with soldiers to battlefields. But Khurram and Mumtaz were too much in love to ever be parted. Mumtaz was always with her husband, even when the danger was very great. In their first seven years of marriage, she gave birth to seven children—most of them while she was in a tent close to a battlefield.

Mumtaz, however, was not roughing it. Her tent was not the kind you bring on a camping trip. It was huge and had many comforts. The royal tent was surrounded by wooden panels decorated with scarlet cloth. It had many halls, including one for Mumtaz and her attendants. In another, Khurram received visits from his officers and advisors. Chefs prepared meals in special ovens. Lamps burning a mix of cotton seed and oil lit up the night. Singers, dancers, and musicians provided entertainment. There were two of these royal tents. Early each morning, servants would ride ahead to the next stopping place. There they would set up a new tent for Khurram, Mumtaz, and the rest of the court. By the time the royal party arrived, everything was ready for them.

Khurram was away from the court much of the time. Still he managed to learn of plots against him in Agra.

One of his father's wives had a son that she favored. She tried to get Jahangir to make her son the heir to the throne. Khurram felt that his father was too weak to resist her. So Khurram started a rebellion against his father's rule. It was unsuccessful. Even so, Khurram was able to gain his father's forgiveness—on two conditions. Khurram and Mumtaz were sent away to live in exile. And they also had to leave two of their sons behind as hostages.

The couple was still in exile in 1627, when Jahangir died. The Moguls had a saying: When the ruler died, his sons would fight. They would either "win the throne" (become emperor) or "face the coffin" (die). The soldiers of the army were loyal to Khurram. In a short time he defeated and killed his half brothers.

On January 24, 1628, Khurram entered Agra in triumph. Mumtaz was at his side. It was a splendid parade, with the royal couple and their attendants riding elephants. They scattered coins among the crowds along the way.

Khurram became ruler on February 14. He took the name Shah Jahan. It means "King of the World." Jewels were poured over his head. He gave Mumtaz thousands of gold pieces.

Shah Jahan and Mumtaz moved into the Red Fort, which he began to expand and improve. She became his closest advisor and was trusted with the royal seal. The seal was used like a stamp of approval. It gave her the power to look over and okay documents.

Shah Jahan had other wives, but Mumtaz was his favorite. A historian of the time said that Shah Jahan's love for Mumtaz "exceeded by a thousand times what he felt for any other." He called Mumtaz "the companion, close confidante, associate and intimate friend of that successful ruler, in hardship and comfort, joy and grief, when traveling or in residence." She used her power behind the scenes. Her husband asked her advice on all important decisions. Because Mumtaz always remembered to help the poor, the people loved her.

By Shah Jahan's time, Agra was a wonder of Asia. The city was a meeting place for scholars, writers, and religious leaders. A European visitor who saw Agra during Shah Jahan's rule described it as one of the biggest cities in the world. Gardens lined the many mansions on the banks of the Yamuna River.

Shah Jahan held court twice a day. Common people could come to ask favors from him. Every morning he appeared at a window in the wall of the fort so that people could see he was alive. On his birthday he had himself weighed four times. The first time, the scales were balanced against an equal amount of silver. The second time, against gold and precious stones. The third time, against cloth woven with gold, silver, and silk. Finally, against a variety of foods. All of these were then given out to the people. No wonder he was a popular ruler.

The Peacock Throne

When Shah Jahan began his rule, he ordered a magnificent throne. Because it was decorated with peacocks, it became known as the Peacock Throne.

Many Muslims believed peacocks guarded the gateway to Heaven. Because Shah Jahan claimed to speak with the voice of God, his throne was like Heaven. A motto was inscribed on the back of the throne: "If there is a paradise on earth, it is here, it is here."

A cushion rested on a platform eight feet long and six feet wide. Surrounding it were twelve pillars that supported a dome that rose twelve feet above the floor.

No expense was spared in making the throne. The twelve pillars were made of solid gold. In all, more than 2,500 pounds of gold were used to construct

the throne. Diamonds, rubies, emeralds, and pearls decorated it inside and out.

CHAPTER 4
Tragedy

In the late spring of 1631, Shah Jahan went to war against the governor of one of the provinces. The governor had started a rebellion. The battlefield was in an area called the Deccan plain, in the south. As always, Mumtaz traveled with her husband, although she was expecting their fourteenth child.

Weather in the Deccan is usually very hot. Temperatures often rise over 100 degrees Fahrenheit. The land there is dusty and dry. When Mumtaz was about to give birth, she moved to a fortress overlooking a river. The air would be cooler there. She and the baby would be safe.

On June 16, Shah Jahan's troops won a victory. Joyfully, he went to the fortress to tell his wife the good news.

But Mumtaz was near death! She had already gone into labor. And it was taking too long for the baby to be born. She was exhausted from the pain and the heat. She told a doctor that she heard the baby within her crying. That was supposed to be a bad omen.

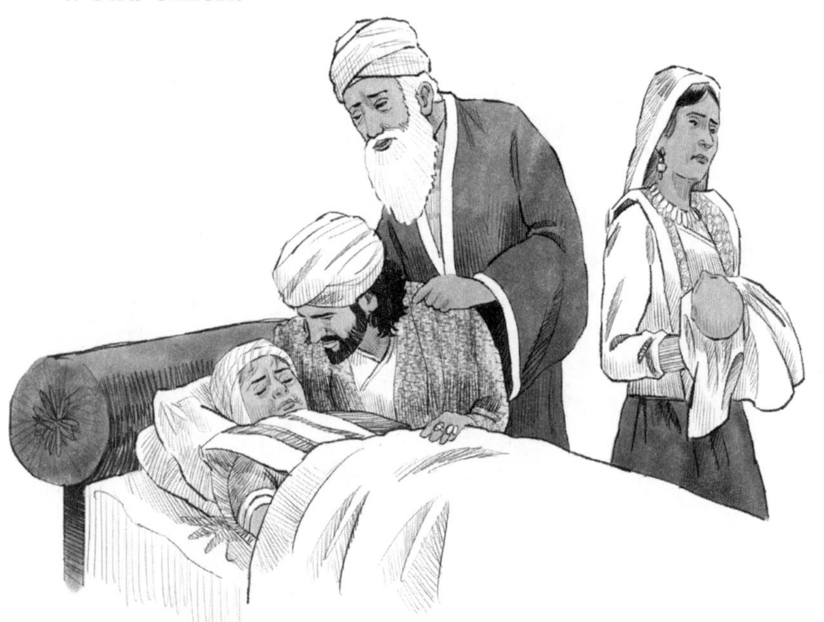

Finally, after thirty hours, she gave birth to a daughter. The doctor feared that Mumtaz would not survive. The doctor was right.

Shah Jahan came to his wife's side. She told him that this was "the time of departure." She said that she had dreamed of a beautiful palace with a lush garden, the like of which she had never imagined. She asked Jahan to build a tomb like that for her. She wanted it to be so perfect, it would be like Heaven on earth.

She died in his arms as the sun rose the next day.

By Muslim custom, a dead person is buried within twenty-four hours. So Mumtaz's body was laid to rest in a garden near the fortress. Shah Jahan put on white clothes (the color of mourning) and shut himself inside a tent. Eight days later, he reappeared. His beard and hair had turned white, even though he was only thirty-nine.

Returning home, he declared a time of mourning, when everyone had to grieve for Mumtaz. It lasted two years. Almost everyone

wore white during that time. Music, perfume, cosmetics, jewelry, and colorful clothing were forbidden. Anyone who didn't abide by these rules could be put to death.

In December 1631, Shah Jahan ordered one of his sons to bring the body of Mumtaz back to Agra. The prince did as his father wished. He led a parade of elephants, carrying his mother's

body in a golden coffin. All along the way, coins and food were given out to people in need. These gifts were in memory of Mumtaz, who had always shown concern for the poor.

The procession reached Agra in early January. For now, the body was buried near the Yamuna River. Every Wednesday—the day of the week on which Mumtaz died—Shah Jahan visited the grave. This spot by the river would be the right place, he decided, to build her magnificent tomb.

CHAPTER 5
A Plan

Shah Jahan wanted the tomb of his beloved to overlook the Yamuna River. The owner of the land offered it to Shah Jahan for free. But instead, the Shah gave him a palace.

Even before the plans for the building were completed, work started. Water would be an important part of the tomb area. There would be channels and fountains.

Building near a river presented problems. Part of the year India has a season of heavy rains, called *monsoons*. The building for the tomb had to be protected from flooding. It also had to be kept from sinking into the soft ground.

Hundreds of workers began digging a huge foundation. Shah Jahan wanted it finished as soon as possible. So they worked even in the hottest time of the year. Sometimes the temperature reached 110 degrees Fahrenheit.

Drainage pipes and channels were installed. They were encased in stone and mortar. There may be more than a thousand such pipes in the foundation. Then the entire foundation was filled with stone to bring it up to ground level.

Architects began designing the tomb at once. Shah Jahan brought artists and master builders from all over Asia. There is no one person who gets credit for designing the Taj Mahal. Shah Jahan was himself interested in architecture, and he probably supervised the entire project.

The Taj is no ordinary building, and Shah Jahan had to be patient. More than twenty thousand workers and craftsmen labored on the memorial for nearly twenty-two years. Most of them were Hindus. They needed a place to live, and a city was built for them south of the construction site. It was named after Mumtaz.

Countless caravans of carts brought food and construction materials to the site. Warehouses were built to store them. Visitors came, too,

because they wanted to see the wondrous project being built. Lodging had to be provided for these people.

Most large buildings in Mogul India—like the Red Fort, for instance—were made from red sandstone. However, Mumtaz's final resting place had to be special. The main tomb and the massive platform on which it stood were to be made of marble.

The marble came from far away. There was a quarry at Makrana, more than two hundred miles to the west. Shah Jahan ordered that all the marble from there was to be used for the tomb.

A European priest who visited Agra wrote, "[Blocks of white marble] had been brought there from over forty leagues away. . . . Some of these blocks, which I met on the way . . . were of such unusual size and length that they drew the sweat of many powerful teams of oxen and of

fierce-looking, big-horned buffaloes, which were dragging enormous, strongly made wagons, in teams of twenty or thirty animals."

At that time, construction workers climbed scaffolds made of bamboo to do their jobs. Because the stone for the tomb was so heavy, this scaffold had to be made of bricks.

When the construction project was completed, Shah Jahan was told it would take five years to take apart the scaffold. Instead he offered the bricks to anyone who would take them. They disappeared overnight.

Once the marble reached the site, it was too heavy to be lifted by the workers. Instead, ramps of earth were built, and workers used ropes with pulleys to drag the heavy stone to the topmost level under construction. Probably oxen and even elephants were used to help. It is thought that the dome of the Taj Mahal alone weighs more than twelve thousand tons. That is equal to about twenty-five jet airliners.

Hundreds of skilled masons were called on to fit the stones together. The masons smoothed the places where each stone met another. Their work was so precise that a historian of the time wrote that no one could see "any cracks between [the stones]." In some parts of the monument, red sandstone was used. Afterward, the masons covered the sandstone with white marble.

In June 1632, a year after Mumtaz died, a memorial service called an *Urs* was held at the construction site. From then on, each year on the anniversary of her death, an Urs took place. It was a way to honor the memory of Mumtaz and keep her alive in the minds of the people.

The occasion was somber but very lavish. Tents were raised in the gardens. On carpets inside,

people could enjoy food, beverages, and sweets. Spices and perfumes freshened the air.

Many people gathered for the Urs. A British diplomat wrote, "All the face of the earth, so far as we could see, was covered with people, troops of horses, elephants with innumerable flags . . . which made a most gallant show."

Shah Jahan appeared in his white robes of mourning. After listening to prayers, he retired to his private rooms in the Red Fort. He was still grieving.

CHAPTER 6
The Plan Grows Larger

As the work continued, Shah Jahan's vision became bigger. The tomb building would be part of a much larger complex. The grand mausoleum (the building containing the body of Mumtaz) would be at the center of everything.

The mausoleum was to sit on a platform, or *plinth*. It measured 312 square feet and was twenty-three feet high. The building would be topped by an immense white marble dome shaped like a giant pearl.

On top of the dome was a *finial*, a rod with three globes and a crescent moon, a symbol of Islam. The three globes represent animals, humans, and angels. (Originally the finial was made of gold,

finial

but it has been replaced by one of gilded bronze.)

The shape of the building itself formed a square with flattened corners that turned it into an octagon. At each of the four corners of the mausoleum there was to be a 130-foot-high minaret. (*Minarets* are towers that Muslim religious leaders climb to call the faithful to prayer.) The minarets on the Taj Mahal were made to lean slightly outward so that if they ever fell, they would not harm the building.

Around the main dome there would be four smaller domes, each the same shape as the main one. Niches and false doorways around the sides of the building repeated the design of the central doorway.

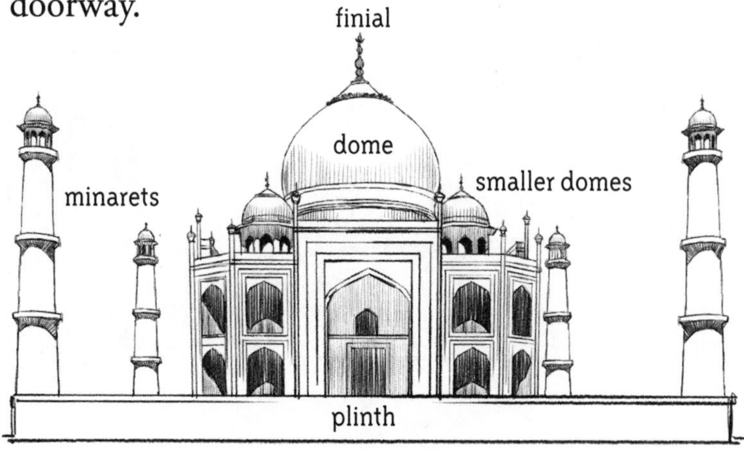

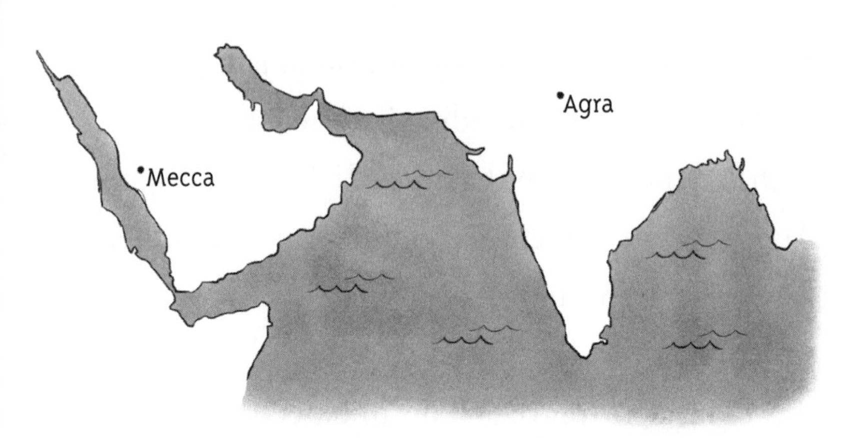

Mumtaz would be buried inside in the exact center. According to Islamic law, her body had to lie with her face turned westward toward Mecca, Islam's holiest city. All Muslims turn toward it when they pray.

Shah Jahan wanted the complex to be so wonderful that many people would come to visit. So to the west of the mausoleum he planned a mosque made of red sandstone. The floor would be covered with the outlines of 569 prayer rugs in black marble. (Muslims use rugs to kneel on when they pray.)

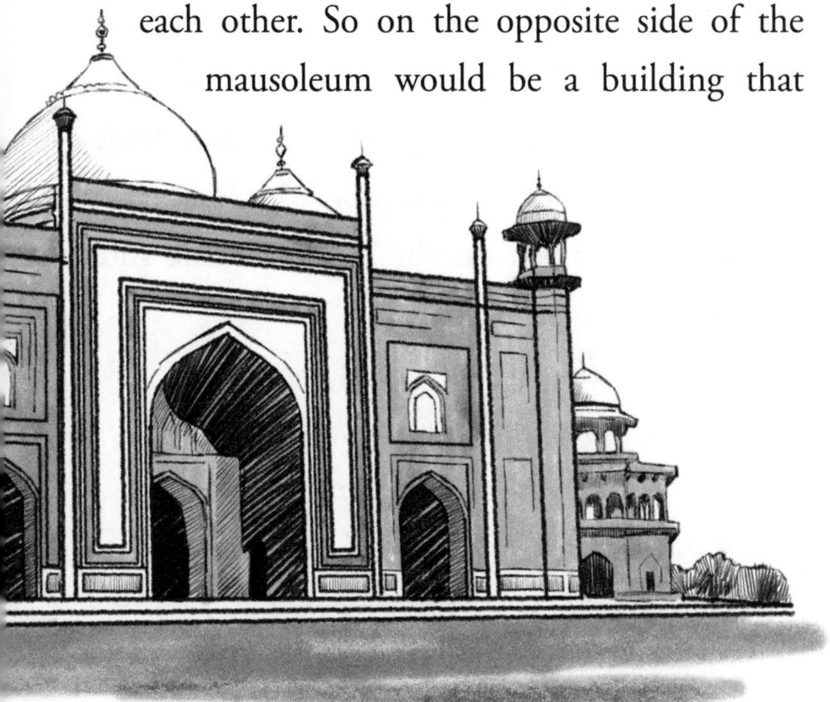

Everything in the complex had to be symmetrical—that means the two sides mirror each other. So on the opposite side of the mausoleum would be a building that looked just like the red sandstone mosque. It was to serve as a place for important guests to stay. The guest house became known as the mosque's *jahab*, or "echo." Both of the red sandstone buildings would have domes exactly half as high as the tomb's dome.

The tomb was going to be beautiful beyond compare. But the view from it was also very important. The Taj would look down onto a walled garden. This garden was to reflect the Muslim idea of Paradise. Shah Jahan recalled his wife's dying wish, and declared, "May the Abode [home] of Mumtaz be Paradise." He even had a message inscribed on the red sandstone gate leading into the Taj Mahal.

But O thou soul at peace,
Return thou unto thy Lord, well-pleased,
and well-pleasing unto Him,
Enter thou among My servants
And enter thou My Paradise.

CHAPTER 7
Jewels and More Jewels

The twelfth Urs took place when Mumtaz's tomb was completed. That was in 1643. It was already a beautiful sight. But Shah Jahan was not satisfied. He wanted it to be even more spectacular. It had to be decorated the way he imagined Heaven to look.

Shah Jahan loved jewelry of all kinds. He designed jewelry himself, and paintings show him wearing it on his body and his turban. He used a string of perfect pearls as prayer beads.

He wanted the walls of the Taj Mahal to shine with jewels. Throughout the building are precious and semi-precious stones.

The most common designs are flowers that are made of tiny jewels. Shah Jahan's favorite flower

was a tulip, and there are many of them on the walls.

A craftsman would use a grinding wheel to make an outline of the flower in the marble. Then he cut pieces of gems to fit into the space perfectly. A kind of glue was used to hold the pieces in place. The surface of the flower was polished so that the lines between pieces became invisible.

Some of the jeweled tulips are amazingly detailed. As many as sixty pieces of stone are used to make a flower only one inch high.

Larger spaces on the walls are covered by many flowers on stems that form an elaborate design. There are also raised decorations of flowers made from polished white plaster. The plaster is so smooth that it is hard to tell it from marble.

Also inlaid on the walls is *calligraphy*—fancy writing. Most are quotes from the Koran, Islam's holy book. No ink was used. All of the calligraphy is made of black marble. Calligraphy is important to Muslims because words of the Koran are sacred.

The person who designed the quotes in the Taj Mahal received a special honor. His name, Amanat Khan Shirazi, is the only one to appear on the tomb. The name meant "Lord of Trust," and was given to him by Shah Jahan.

Lamps and candlesticks were also created to light the inside of the tomb and other buildings. Originally, there were carpets and cushions on the floors. These no longer exist.

When all the decorative work was finished, it was time to work on the waterways and gardens outside. These would complete the Muslim idea of Paradise.

CHAPTER 8
The Gardens

The English word *paradise* comes from the Persian word *pairidaeza*, which means a "walled garden." Think about it. A garden with a wall surrounding it is a peaceful and safe place. Like paradise.

Water is a very important part of all Islamic gardens. The Koran tells of four rivers in Paradise. Thus the garden at the Taj Mahal was divided into four parts by streams of water. At the center, where the streams met, was a large, square white-marble pool with fountains. This pool represented the place where the human and the divine meet. At each end of the east-west channel, platforms were built where musicians would play.

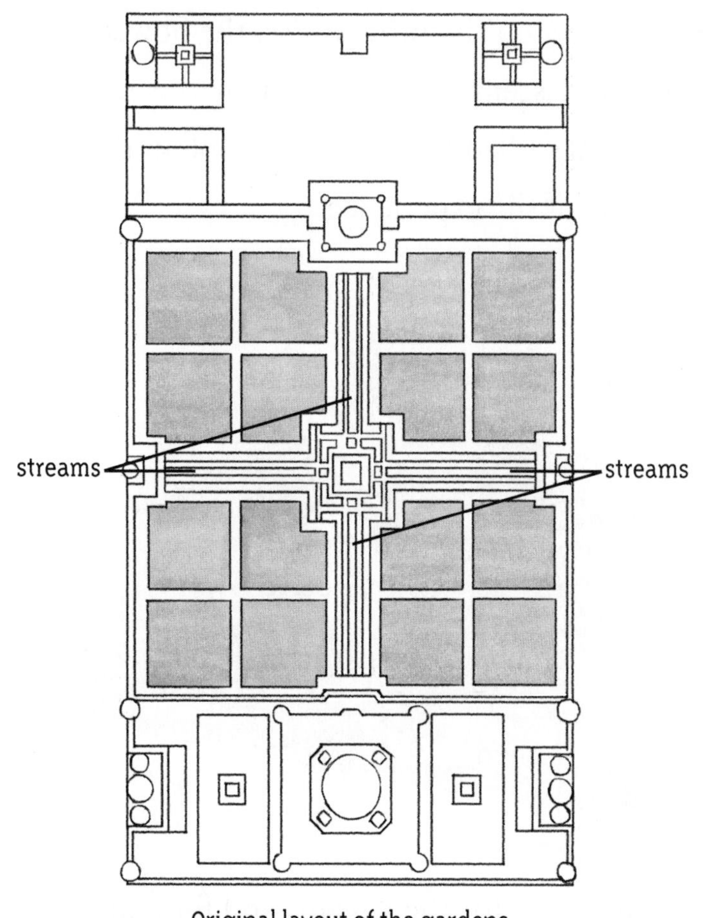

Original layout of the gardens

The four squares made by the streams of water were planted with trees and flowers. The trees were chosen for their shade and aroma.

Fruits grew on them. Likewise, the flowers added color and scent. Birds nested in the trees, and their songs filled the air. The use of all the senses was part of the experience.

The water for the streams and fountains came from the Yamuna River. Bringing it to the complex required clever engineering. That's because the Yamuna is lower than the ground on which the Taj Mahal was built.

First, engineers had to channel river water into a settlement tank. Here silt and other debris would sink to the bottom, purifying the water.

Then a system of thirteen *purs* brought the water up to a brick aqueduct. A pur consisted of a large roller with a rope around it. The rope was attached to a leather bucket. A pair of oxen turned the roller, pulling the bucket upward. The water inside was dumped into another tank, with another pur, and so on until it reached the level of the Taj Mahal. From there it was directed into the streams around the garden.

When visitors passed through the entrance gate, they saw the great white dome of the Taj Mahal twice. First, the dome itself, and then its reflection in the pool of water in front. The carefully planned sight was so stunning that people stopped in their tracks to stare at it. Tourists today do the same thing.

CHAPTER 9
Imprisoned

Perhaps the memories of Mumtaz became too painful for Shah Jahan to remain at the building site. Although the Taj Mahal was not finished, in 1639, he began work on a city named after him: Shahjahanabad. It was located about forty miles from Agra, on the west bank of the Yamuna River. A town named Delhi had already existed there.

The primary building in the new city was a new Red Fort. It was twice as large as the one in Agra. It was like a city in itself. Circled by a high

red sandstone wall and a moat, it had twenty-seven towers and eleven great gates. Inside were grand avenues, markets, shops, courtiers' homes, government buildings, and pavilions decorated with gold and jewels. The emperor and his family lived in a private palace within the fort.

A French visitor described it: "Nearly every chamber has its reservoir of running water at the door; on every side are gardens, delightful alleys, shady retreats, streams, fountains, grottoes, deep excavations that afford shelter from the sun by day . . . [and] terraces on which to sleep coolly at night. Within the walls of this enchanting place, no oppressive or inconvenient heat is felt."

The new Red Fort

In 1648, to the beating of kettledrums, Shah Jahan arrived at the fort by boat and mounted his Peacock Throne. He was at the height of his power. He had not forgotten Mumtaz. Taxes on nearby villages were spent to complete the work on the Taj Mahal and keep it in good condition.

But the Taj Mahal, the fort, and other building projects had drained the royal treasury. Unsuccessful wars added to the strains on the empire. After Shah Jahan fell ill in 1657, his four sons fought for control.

The winner was Aurangzeb, who defeated and executed all of his brothers. He declared himself emperor. When Shah Jahan recovered from his illness, he tried to take back the throne. But Aurangzeb would not give up power. He said Shah Jahan was not fit to rule and imprisoned him in the Red Fort in Agra.

Shah Jahan lived there for eight years, until his death in 1666. From the fort, he could gaze upon the monument he had built for his wife.

Shah Jahan died reciting verses from the Koran. During his last days, servants placed a mirror so he could see the Taj Mahal from his bed. Aurangzeb had him buried in the Taj Mahal, next to his beloved Mumtaz. Shah Jahan's coffin and sarcophagus are the only parts of the structure that are not symmetrical with the rest.

Tourists Today

Today at the Taj Mahal, visitors climb steps to the plinth and then enter the main doorway. Inside, natural light pours in through windows high above. A large lamp also hangs from the dome. (It was added later.) The inside of the dome is smaller than the dome outside. It was made this way to create more pleasing proportions for the interior.

Most of the interior is a sanctuary (a sacred place) surrounded by a white-marble screen, six feet tall. The screen is carved in such detail that it looks like lace.

Inside the sanctuary are two *cenotaphs.* (A cenotaph is a box that looks like a coffin but does not contain a body.) However, they only represent the resting place for Mumtaz and Shah Jahan. A flight of stairs leads down to a dark chamber that holds the coffins with their bodies. No one is allowed to go there.

Inscribed on the wall of the tomb is Shah Jahan's sorrowful prayer: "Help us, O Lord, to bear that which we cannot bear." What he could not bear was the loss of his beloved Mumtaz.

CHAPTER 10
Decline

Over time, the Taj Mahal has suffered from decay, vandalism, and neglect. For a monument where water is so important, leakage has been a terrible problem. Even while Shah Jahan was still alive, his son sent reports to him in jail on what was being done to repair leaks.

Foreign invaders weakened the power of the Moguls. In 1739, Nadir Shah of Persia invaded India and took the Peacock Throne back home. Eight years later he was murdered and his assassins broke up the throne.

Europeans began to establish powerful colonies in India. In 1608, a company in Great Britain first sent trading missions to India. By 1757, the company—the British East India Company—

had become the actual ruler of much of India, which had no central government.

The British had no respect for the historical monuments that the Indian people had built. Even the Taj Mahal was not valued for its beauty. A proposal was made to take apart the building and ship the marble to England. Fortunately, the plan proved too costly and was never carried out.

Local people didn't treat the Taj Mahal with respect either. In 1754, looters broke into the tombs under the sanctuary and stripped them of all their gold and jewels. People used the Taj Mahal for dances and picnics. Many of the precious stones in the marble walls were chipped out and stolen.

In 1857, a rebellion called the Sepoy Mutiny broke out against the British East India Company. By this time, the Company had its own army. British soldiers harshly put down the rebels. And the last of the Mogul rulers was exiled. The Company destroyed much of the inside of the Red Fort in Delhi and used it as an army barracks.

However, the days of the Company's power were coming to an end. The British government took over the Company and what it owned.

Queen Victoria of England took the title Empress of India. In 1912, Delhi (formerly Shahjahanabad) became the capital of British-ruled India.

Queen Victoria

During this time, the British tried to show they were good rulers by restoring some of India's monuments. The Taj was one. The British, however, were fond of lawns. They planted grass in the gardens where flowers and fruit trees once grew. This was not the paradise that Shah Jahan had envisioned.

CHAPTER 11
The Pride of Modern India

In 1947, India became independent. British rule was over. There was a ceremony at Shah Jahan's Red Fort at Delhi. It was a time of great hope and pride for the people of India.

The country was going to be a democracy with leaders that the people elected. The magnificent Taj Mahal was a symbol of the new country's pride. A prize-winning Indian poet had written of the Taj Mahal:

You knew, Emperor of India, Shah Jahan,
That life, youth, wealth, renown
All float away down the stream of time . . .
Yet still one solitary tear
Would hang on the cheek of time
In the form
Of this white and gleaming Taj Mahal.

The new Indian government continued efforts started by the British to care for famous

landmarks. But the nation had many needs that had to come before restoring old buildings. So many of India's people were poor and hungry. Better ways of farming had to be developed. Factories also needed to be built.

However, it soon became clear that the Taj Mahal was a great tourist attraction. Visitors from all over the world came to see it. They spent money that helped the economy of India.

That convinced the government to step up efforts to restore the Taj Mahal. Its goal was to make the building look the way it had originally. Historians searched for documents about the construction of the building and its gardens. Scientists tried to determine exactly what kinds of plants had been in the gardens.

In 1983, an agency of the United Nations (UNESCO) put the Taj Mahal and the Red Fort of Agra on its list of World Heritage Sites. This helped get more money to restore the Taj Mahal.

World Heritage Sites

UNESCO (United Nations Educational, Scientific, and Cultural Organization) has created a list of World Heritage Sites. These are more than a thousand places that are particularly important in world culture. Some, like the Taj Mahal, were made by humans. Others, such as the Grand Canyon, are natural formations.

There are twenty-three World Heritage Sites in the United States. They range from the Hawaii Volcanoes National Park to the Statue of Liberty. Canada has seventeen sites, and India has thirty-two. Besides the Taj Mahal, those related to events in this book are the Red Fort in Agra and the Red Fort in Delhi.

The money was badly needed. By the end of the 1900s, parts of the Taj Mahal were starting to look rundown. Agra was now a large industrial city. Factories poured out smoke and dirt particles. They were discoloring the white marble of the Taj Mahal. As in many countries, greater use of automobiles caused pollution.

Adding to the problem were fires made from charcoal and dung that poor people in the area still used to cook their food.

Now there are several anti-pollution efforts to protect the Taj Mahal. Only lead-free gasoline is sold in Agra. People now must cook with propane.

Between two and three million people visit the Taj Mahal every year. Most of them are from India. Tourism is a good thing. But it is also a bad thing because huge crowds cause some damage to the monument. Today, gasoline-powered vehicles are not allowed within 550 yards of the Taj Mahal. Visitors must ride electric-powered buses or carts drawn by animals.

To restore the original color of the Taj Mahal, a special mud pack is applied to the stone from time to time. This is followed by a "bath" of pure water. An enormous scaffold has to be built for the job.

In 1999, India went to war with the neighboring country of Pakistan. Would the Taj Mahal become a target of the enemy? Two years later, to protect the monument, local tailors sewed a massive black camouflage net and draped it over the building. This hid the Taj Mahal from enemy bombers. Though the Taj Mahal was not actually attacked, the effort to save it showed how devoted Indians are to their most famous building.

CHAPTER 12
More Discoveries

Something puzzled art scholars until recently. In Islamic tomb gardens, the mausoleum usually sits at the place where the water channels meet. But the Taj Mahal does not fit that pattern. The tomb is at the far end.

In the 1990s, scientists began to dig in the area across the river from the Taj Mahal. They cleared away silt and weeds that had grown there from centuries of flooding. Underneath they discovered something wonderful—the remnants of a magnificent garden.

Like the one at the Taj Mahal, it too once had walkways, pavilions, pools, fountains, trees, and flowers. A wall made of brick, plaster, and red sandstone surrounded the garden. Four sandstone towers stood at the corners.

This was a "moonlight garden," where the view of the Taj Mahal was best at night. The Yamuna River itself was part of this view, reflecting the light of the moon. The dome of the Taj Mahal, even today, shines brightly in the full moon. The flowers that were planted on this side were mostly white ones. They were chosen because they released their aroma at night.

This discovery proved that the mausoleum was exactly halfway between the end of this garden and the entrance to the whole complex. Just as people had suspected, the mausoleum itself was intended to be the center of a single huge monument.

Today, the night garden across the river, like the one at the Taj Mahal entrance, is being restored. There are eighty-one different kinds of flowers, all known to have been favorites of the Moguls. At night, Shah Jahan liked to view the monument from here.

When the moon is full and the sky is clear, the Taj Mahal still seems to shimmer just the way it did in his time, three and a half centuries ago.

Myths of the Taj Mahal

Ever since the Taj Mahal was built, myths about it have spread. The most common one is that Shah Jahan intended to build an identical tomb, made of black stone, for himself. As the story goes, he wasn't able to do that because his son took him prisoner.

The overall design of the Taj Mahal complex shows that Shah Jahan probably didn't plan a second tomb. The discovery of a moonlight garden on the other side of the river shows that the white-domed tomb was the center of a symmetrical complex. Putting a second tomb in the complex would have spoiled that plan.

Another myth is that the workers on the Taj Mahal had their hands cut off. This was supposed to guarantee that they couldn't build anything else as grand. The story is not true. Shah Jahan had other building projects. Finding workers to do those jobs

would have been difficult if that was the "reward" for doing a good job!

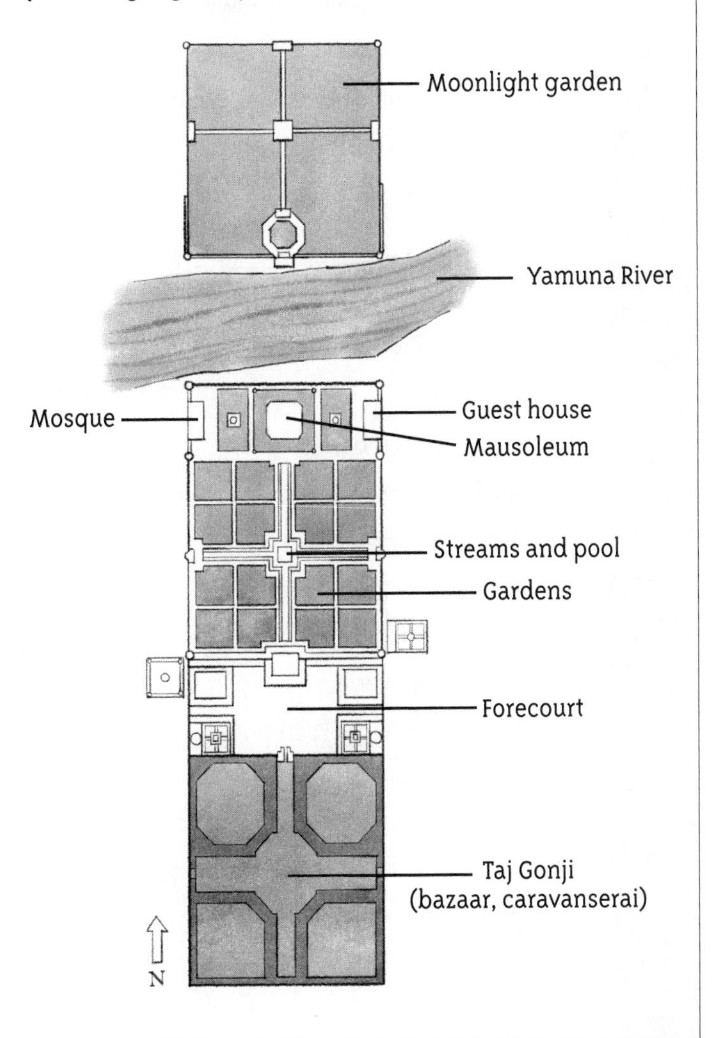

Timeline of the Taj Mahal

1526	Beginning of Mogul Empire in India
1556	Akbar the Great becomes emperor
1592	Khurram, the future Shah Jahan, is born
1607	Khurram meets Mumtaz Mahal
1612	Wedding of Khurram and Mumtaz Mahal
1631	Mumtaz Mahal dies
1632	Construction on the Taj Mahal begins
1658	Aurangzeb displaces his father, becomes emperor
1666	Shah Jahan dies
1869	Mahatma Gandhi is born
1877	Queen Victoria becomes Empress of India
1947	India becomes independent
1983	Declared UNESCO World Heritage Site
1990s	Remnants of Mehtab Bagh (Moonlight Garden) discovered on other side of river
1998	India's Supreme Court orders anti-pollution measures to protect building from deterioration
1999	Indo-Pakistani war, Taj is camouflaged
2007	Chosen as one of New Seven Wonders of the World by millions of voters around the world

Timeline of the World

1504	Michelangelo sculpts *David*
1600	English East India Company established
1610	Galileo sees moons of Jupiter through his telescope
1619	Dutch ship brings first African slaves to North America
1620	Pilgrims land at Plymouth Rock
1642	English Civil War begins
1644	End of Ming Dynasty in China
1661	Building of the Palace of Versailles begins in France
1837	Victoria becomes queen of Great Britain
1885	World's first skyscraper built in Chicago
1945	The United Nations founded
1971	India goes to war with Pakistan, helps Bangladesh win independence
1985	Ronald Reagan sworn in as US president for second term
1991	Persian Gulf War between the United States and Iraq
2010	Burj Khalifa in Dubai becomes tallest building in the world

Bibliography

***Books for young readers**

*DuTemple, Lesley A. ***The Taj Mahal***. Minneapolis: Lerner Publications, 2003.

Edwards, Mike. "'Paradise on Earth': When the Moguls Ruled India." ***National Geographic*** 167, no. 4 (April 1985): 462–93.

Gascoigne, Bamber. ***A Brief History of the Great Moguls: India's Most Flamboyant Rulers***. New York: Carroll and Graf, 2002.

*Henzel, Cynthia Kennedy. ***Taj Mahal***. Edina, MN: ABDO Publishing, 2011.

Koch, Ebba. ***The Complete Taj Mahal and the Riverfront Gardens of Agra***. London: Thames and Hudson, 2006.

*Mann, Elizabeth. ***Taj Mahal***. New York: Mikaya Press, 2008.

Preston, Diana, and Michael Preston. ***Taj Mahal: Passion and Genius at the Heart of the Moghul Empire***. New York: Walker & Co., 2007.

Sen Gupta, Subhadra. ***Taj Mahal: Agra and Fatehpur Sikri***. New Delhi: Prakash Books, 2006.

Williams, A.R. "Rescuing an Icon." ***National Geographic*** 228, no. 2 (August 2015).